Role models for women who se... ...ove of Jesus

the three Marys

BIBLE STUDY

Role models for women who seek the love of Jesus

the three Marys

BIBLE STUDY

Eva J. Gibson

AMG
Publishers

First Printing, April 2012

Print Edition	ISBN 13: 978-0-89957-347-2	ISBN 10: 0-89957-347-9
EPUB Edition	ISBN 13: 978-1-61715-406-5	ISBN 10: 1-61715-406-7
Mobi Edition	ISBN 13: 978-1-61715-407-2	ISBN 10: 1-61715-407-5
E-PDF Edition	ISBN 13: 978-1-61715-408-9	ISBN 10: 1-61715-408-3

Edited by Diane Stortz and Rick Steele

Layout by Adept Content Solutions, Urbana, Illinois

Front cover design by Taylor Ware, InView Graphics, Chattanooga, Tennessee

Cover layout by Michael Largent, InView Graphics, Chattanooga, Tennessee

Printed in the United States of America
16 15 14 13 12 11 –V– 6 5 4 3 2 1

Contents

Introduction

Women need women to model what it means to be women of God. However, many women today live far from the families, churches, and communities where they grew up. Frequent moves of their own hinder the building of godly relationships with other women. And that isn't all. Some have never experienced family life as God originally intended. They don't know what it means to be a godly woman.

God anticipated the needs of the women of the twenty-first century. That's one of the reasons He gave us the three Marys—Jesus's mother, Mary Magdalene, and Mary of Bethany. These women were closely connected to Jesus's life and ministry when He was on earth. They ate with Him, walked with Him, and listened to His words. Yet as we study the lives of these women, we will see ourselves in them—ordinary women who struggled and cried and loved just like we do. You will meet . . .

- *Mary the mother of Jesus*. By saying yes to God, trusting His character, and coping with God-ordained change, this Mary gave us an example of obedience and courage.
- *Mary Magdalene, a woman with a painful past*. Her story allows us to focus on the deliverance Christ offers and the transformed life that results when we appropriate His forgiveness as our own.
- *Mary of Bethany*. She sat at the feet of Jesus as a disciple. More than anything, she just wanted to spend time with Jesus. Because she did, she understood His heart. The perfume she poured on His head and feet before His death was a memorial of love poured out.

Women have been given a unique ministry of comfort. These women inspire us with their raw courage and their willingness to be there for the Lord they loved during His crucifixion. Mary Magdalene was one of the women who went to the garden to anoint Jesus's body. When Jesus appeared to her, He told her to take the message of His resurrection to the men. It's the message Christians have been given to take to the world.

After the ascension the women waited in the upper room as Jesus told them to. God always keeps His promises to those who quietly wait. That's something we need to discover too.

Each woman had problems and joys; it is the richness of each character and the diversity of each life that made each one unique. As you study and discuss the ways each woman related to Jesus, you will find yourself in one of them—or in a combination of all three. You will see more clearly the woman God longs for you to be. With His help you will become that woman.

Overview of the Study

Each lesson in this study includes these four parts:

- "A Closer Look at the Problem" defines the problem and the goal of the lesson.
- "A Closer Look at God's Word" gets you into God's Word. What does God have to say about the problem? How can you begin to apply God's Word as you work through the Scriptures?
- "A Closer Look at My Life" will help you clarify and further apply truth.
- "Action Steps I Can Take Today" is designed to help you concentrate on immediate and practical steps of action.

You Will Need

Plan ahead to get the full benefit of this study. Secure the following before you begin:

- A Bible.
- A notebook. Each study has suggestions for journaling, especially in the "Action Steps I Can Take Today" section. You may also wish to journal additional thoughts and feelings as you look closely at the lives of the three Marys. Journaling is a great tool to help you think things through with God.
- You will also need time to savor what you're learning, time to ponder the deep things of God as Mary, Jesus's mother, did after the birth of her Son. "Mary treasured up all these things and pondered them in her heart" (Luke 2:19).

Mary, Jesus's Mother

A Woman Who Knew God's Heart

In the winter, stores display boxes of holiday cards celebrating the season. Some cards hone in on Santa Claus, candles, and winter landscapes; a few include nativity scenes.

Joseph stands holding his staff in his hand. Mary kneels beside him, personifying a lovely young mother, oval face partially obscured by the mantel she wears, dark hair escaping around the edges. A new-mommy look radiates from her as she looks down at the newborn either nestled in her arms or enfolded in cloths tucked inside a manger.

Our world tries to wipe out the Christ child, but to us who believe, He is the glory of Christmas and rightfully so. We need to be reminded in celebration and song of the night our redeemer was born into a world obscured by the dark shadow of the Roman empire.

But wait! Let's not miss this woman God chose to love and nurture His Son. What was she like? How did she think? What kind of world did she live in? Most important, what can women of the twenty-first century and beyond learn from her?

It isn't easy to cope with the darkness of our world or even the darkness in our individual lives. Nor is it easy to face the changes that inevitably come as we live our lives, day by day.

The goal of this week's study is to take a close look in Scripture at Mary, the mother of Jesus, to see how she, as a young woman, chose to trust God. Just as Mary's heart was turned toward her Messiah, so can your heart be turned toward God as you study His Word. The promised one is about to come. Mary had been chosen to be His mother. You have been chosen to discover and learn truth you can apply to your life.

A Closer Look at the Problem

The World into Which Mary Was Born

Mary's world was a world of uncertainty and darkness. Her beloved Palestine was controlled by Rome, a powerful and cruel empire that extended from Asia, around the Mediterranean Sea to the far-off Atlantic Ocean in the west.

Although Rome had left much of the government in the hands of the local people, Roman officials were everywhere in Israel. Their presence was seen and felt daily as they maintained tight control, either through direct rule or through loyal servants in distant outposts.

Some Jews had withdrawn and put all their energy into observing the Jewish law. Others had revolted by trying to overthrow Rome. Claiming to be the Messiah, they were crucified one after another and left to rot on Roman crosses placed alongside the roads.

The armies of the empire conquered many lands. Once conquered, they established miniature versions of Rome, with fortresses and strongholds at strategic points. Commerce and materialism infiltrated even the remote villages. At the same time, many Jews resisted this influence. Those who disregarded the effect on their culture underestimated Rome's immense power and authority.

This was the world of Mary's day.

The Family into Which Mary Was Born

Even though Mary lived during a time of turmoil and unrest, she had the love and security of a close-knit family. Daily she experienced a simple life—family prayers, household tasks, the gathering in of the harvest.

Like every devout Jewish woman of that time, she looked forward to the coming of the Messiah, the promised one. She knew from the prophecies that He would be born of a virgin, that He would be a descendant of King David.

Mary belonged to that family. Could the honor of being the mother of the Messiah possibly be given to her?

Enter the Angel Gabriel

The very core of Mary's existence was shaken when an angel appeared and greeted her. But the angel said, "Do not be afraid, Mary, you have found favor with God. You will be with child and give birth to a son, and you are to give him the name Jesus" (Luke 2:30–31).

A young woman betrothed to a man, soon to give birth to a baby? Incredible thought. Under Jewish law terrible things happened to women who committed adultery. The law of Moses spoke of stoning and death.

Doubts must have hammered at Mary's heart. Why should the neighbors believe that the baby she would soon nurture in her own body was indeed the promised one? What would her own family think? And Joseph, the man to whom she was betrothed—would he believe her story? Would he understand?

Could Mary risk losing the love and security that surrounded her like a protective blanket? Mary must have considered these possibilities. What effect would the changes she would soon experience have on her life?

1. Take a few moments right now and think about that long-ago world of darkness and turmoil. Find "The Light of the World" in your songbook or hymnal. (If yours doesn't have that particular song, look for one with a message of Jesus as the light.) Read, hum, or softly sing the words. As you do, ask yourself these questions:

How does being in darkness make me feel?

_____

_____

_____

_____

_____

_____

How is the darkness of my world today similar to the darkness of the world into which Jesus was born?

_____

_____

_____

_____

_____

How is it different?

_____

_____

_____

_____

_____

_____

How would I like Almighty God to penetrate that darkness?

_____

_____

_____

_____

_____

_____

_____

_____

_____

_____

_____

_____

_____

_____

_____

_____

_____

_____

_____

_____

_____

_____

_____

_____

_____

_____

_____

A Closer Look at God's Word

2. Read Luke 1:26–38. Describe the scene in your own words.

_____

_____

_____

_____

_____

_____

Pick out a verse that reveals Mary's emotions and a verse (there's more than one) that reveals Mary as a thinker.

_____

_____

_____

_____

_____

_____

What did Gabriel's salutation reveal about Mary's character?

_____

_____

_____

_____

_____

What did God think of her (v. 28)?

_____

_____

_____

_____

_____

_____

_____

Compare verse 28 with Hebrews 13:5. What does it mean to you to have the assurance that God is with you? That if you belong to Him, He will never, ever leave you or forsake you?

_____

_____

_____

_____

_____

_____

What deep truth about himself is God revealing to Mary through the angel's words in Luke 1:35? Underline each name for Jesus and tell how that name pertains to God himself.

_____

_____

_____

_____

_____

_____

What does Mary's response in 1:38 reveal about her relationship with God?

_____

_____

_____

_____

_____

3. Read Luke 1:39–45. How does Mary reveal her humanity in this account?

_____

_____

_____

_____

_____

_____

_____

Why do you think she chose to visit her kinswoman at this particular time?

_____

_____

_____

_____

_____

_____

What did Elizabeth express that would confirm to Mary that God had indeed chosen her for a special task?

_____

_____

_____

_____

_____

_____

How do believing God and experiencing His blessings fit together?

_____

_____

_____

_____

_____

_____

4. Reread Luke 1:26–45. Purposely step out of your perspective, put yourself in Mary's sandals, and become a part of the story. Choose either Mary's meeting with the angel or her visit with Elizabeth and write about it in your journal. But instead of observing the story, pretend that you are Mary. For example: It's nighttime and you've just talked with an angel. The angel has given you an incredible message. What do you feel? What are you thinking? What changes is this pregnancy going to make in your life? Another example: You've met with Elizabeth. You've heard her words. You've sung your song. Describe the scene and your thoughts and feelings.

_____

_____

_____

_____

5. Read Luke 1:46–56. What does Mary's song reveal about her understanding of God? Either jot down or underline at least three truths about who He is.

_____

_____

_____

_____

_____

Verses 46–47 reveal that Mary knew God, verses 48–49 that she was mindful of who she was and what God wanted to do for her, verse 50 that she knew the Word of God and what He would do in the future, verses 51–55 that she also knew what He had done in the past. How well would you say Mary knew God?

_____

_____

_____

_____

_____

_____

_____

_____

_____

_____

_____

_____

_____

_____

_____

_____

_____

A Closer Look at My Life

Life as Mary experienced it before Gabriel came was changed forever when she talked to him! We've already discovered truth in her song that shows how her understanding of God made her willing to trust Him during this time of change and upheaval in her life.

6. No matter where we are in life, change is inevitable. What changes are you facing right now?

_____

_____

_____

_____

_____

_____

How have these changes affected your attitude?

_____

_____

_____

_____

_____

_____

What effect do you want them to have?

_____

_____

_____

_____

_____

_____

_____

_____

_____

_____

_____

7. What truth have you discovered in Mary's story that you can make your own? Truth that will help you face whatever changes you are experiencing right now?

_____

_____

_____

_____

_____

_____

How do you want that truth to impact your life?

_____

_____

_____

_____

_____

_____

_____

_____

_____

_____

_____

_____

_____

_____

_____

_____

_____

_____

_____

Action Steps I Can Take Today

8. Reread Mary's song (Luke 1:46–55). Spend time each morning this week thinking about who God is. Look for truth from a verse from this Scripture portion or an experience wherein He shows himself to you in a special way. Whichever it is, treasure it in your heart. Think deeply about it, then share it with a friend.

9. The greatest need we have is to trust God for salvation. Zechariah said these words about his son, John the Baptist, expressing the song of his heart: "And you my child, will be called a prophet of the Most High; for you will go on before the Lord to prepare the way for him, to give his people the knowledge of salvation through the forgiveness of their sins" (Luke 1:76–77).

Have you experienced this great salvation—the forgiveness of your sins? If you have, write a thank-you letter to God in your journal.

If you haven't yet experienced this salvation, you can do it now:

Read John 3:16. Recognize God's love.

Read Romans 3:23, 6:23. Admit that you are a sinner.

Read Romans 10:9. Confess your sins to God.

Read John 1:12. Invite Jesus into your life; become His child.

10. Mary's encounter with the angel of the Lord resulted in her submitting herself to God's will. Use the following acrostic to help you evaluate your obedience to your Lord. Ask Him to show you any area in your life that you have not yet placed under His control. When He shows it to you, confess it as sin. Ask Him for His help to enable you to be an obedient woman of God.

O bserve God's Word.

B egin each day with Him.

E agerly wait.

D ie to self.

I n everything give thanks.

E very thought captured by Him.

N o selfishness allowed.

C onfess your sins.

E nd each day with Him.

2

Mary, Jesus's Mother

A Woman Who Pondered Life's Meaning

In our last lesson we met Mary, a young woman who knew God intimately, born into a family of humble means. We met her as she talked with the angel Gabriel and later when she visited Elizabeth, her relative.

We heard Mary's song that gave us insight into her relationship with God. She knew Him as Almighty God, the sovereign Lord, the Savior, the one who went to battle for her.

Three months later she returned to Nazareth to await the coming of the baby promised by the angel. Elizabeth's baby, who had moved in Elizabeth's womb the day Mary greeted Elizabeth, was born. The months passed.

Still Mary waited. Although she and Joseph were betrothed, their marriage had not been consummated. Joseph had taken Mary into his home as his wife, "but he had no union with her until she gave birth to a son" (Matthew 1:25).

Joseph and Mary waited together.

A Closer Look at the Problem

A Glimpse into One Woman's Day

It's hard to wait for the birth of a baby.

But Mary had found the key. As she waited, she kept busy. She had to. Neither her parents or Joseph were wealthy. Simple farmers and craftsmen populated Nazareth, and families rose at dawn to do their daily work. Their tasks occupied them until after the evening meal was served and the sun had set.

A typical day for Mary consisted of baking, gardening, grinding grain, and butchering. And then there were the endless chores—fetching the water, cooking, spinning, sewing, sweeping.

Mary's trips outside the home would have been limited to her daily trek to the well for water and to the marketplace for food and supplies. She took her clothes to a stream for washing and spread them out to dry on nearby bushes.

It would have been easy for Mary to focus on the wrong things. After all, she had lots of things to capture her attention and take her energy. Not just work, but the questions and wondering of the townspeople. Not just the gathering of dung to dry as fuel to heat the oven, but the daily struggles with the discomforts of pregnancy. Not just the hard-packed dirt floors and the roof Joseph had to roll after it rained, but the knowledge that other women had it much easier—the wealthy had stone homes, roomy sleeping rooms, and servants and slaves. They also enjoyed the finest wheat in Palestine while the poorer families made their bread from cheap, coarse barley flour. And Nazareth housed the Roman garrison for the northern regions of Galilee. Most Jews would not associate with those who lived in Nazareth, considering them compromisers who consorted with the enemy.

No, Mary's life was far from easy. She who had been chosen to be the mother of the Messiah didn't exactly have it made.

1. Look at your own life. What are some things you do when you're waiting for something or someone? List them here.

_____

_____

_____

_____

_____

_____

_____

_____

2. On a scale of 1 (problem free) to 10 (very difficult), how would you rate Mary's life at this time?

_____

_____

_____

_____

_____

_____

How did Mary respond? Doubts could have crept into her heart. Discontentment. Fear. Resentment even. "God, you said . . ."

But the heavens were silent. There was no angel now. No word. Life went on in its everyday routine.

It can be the same for us. We know that we belong to God, that we are His children, and that we love Him. But right now life is full to the brim, and it's hard to find time to read our Bibles or pray.

It's good to be busy, but it isn't good to be too busy.

Doubts creep into our hearts.

Discontentment.

Fear.

Resentment even. "God, I thought you'd be there for me. That things would be easier. Why don't you do something?" But God is silent. He's there, but you can't feel His presence or hear His voice.

If you've ever been in this place or are there now, this lesson is for you. You can learn from Mary, a woman who kneaded bread dough and washed fleece and took time to know God. A woman who kept lamps burning, dried vegetables and meat, and thought things through with God. A woman who gave birth to a Son in a stable and listened to shepherds and pondered God's ways.

3. Being busy is good, but sometimes we get too busy. Consider your own life. Are you sometimes too busy to ponder God's ways? To read the Bible and pray? Evaluate what keeps you from spending time with your Lord. What are some things you think you might cut out in order to make time for your relationship with God?

_____

_____

_____

_____

Jewish Marriage Customs

We need to go back now and make sure we understand the marriage customs of the Jews; otherwise, we can come to some wrong conclusions.

Marriages in this culture were arranged for individuals by their parents. After a contract was arranged, the individuals were considered married. They did not, however begin to live together; the woman continued to live with her parents, the man with his, for a year. During this time, if the woman was found to be pregnant, the marriage was annulled. If she demonstrated purity, however, the husband would come to her house and lead her back to the home he had prepared for her in a grand, processional march in which the whole town participated. There, in their new home, they would begin to live together as husband and wife.

We see from Matthew's account that Joseph, when told by the angel that the child Mary was carrying was indeed the promised one, violated these customs. Rather than wait for the one-year betrothal period to pass, he immediately brought her into his home. Matthew makes it plain, however—there was no sexual relationship between them until after the birth of Jesus (Matthew 1:24–25).

A Closer Look at God's Truth

After her visit to Elizabeth, Mary returned home to Nazareth. She lived there quietly with Joseph when all of a sudden—crisis. At least it must have seemed that way to Joseph and Mary.

4. Read Luke 2:1–5. What is happening?

_____

_____

_____

_____

_____

_____

What effect does this Roman decree have on Joseph and Mary?

_____

_____

_____

_____

_____

Why?

_____

_____

_____

_____

_____

_____

Why do you think Joseph took Mary with him to Bethlehem?

_____

_____

_____

_____

_____

_____

What concerns do you think Mary might have had about going?

_____

_____

_____

_____

_____

_____

It probably took Joseph and Mary almost a week to make the ninety-mile trip from Nazareth to Bethlehem. The road was rough and filled with other travelers intent on returning to their ancestral homes for the census. As they entered the town, Joseph and Mary likely met a scene of noisy confusion. People jammed the marketplace: uniformed Roman soldiers and officials, Jews from places like Greece and Egypt, aristocrats and peasants, merchants hawking food and provisions. **How do you think Mary would have felt?**

_____

_____

_____

_____

_____

_____

5. Read Luke 2:6–7. The account of the birth of Jesus is brief. Write these verses in your own words.

_____

_____

_____

_____

_____

Consider the following:

A Galilean peasant and his wife traveled to Bethlehem at the decree of the Roman emperor. But whose decree and plan was Joseph really following (Micah 5:2)?

_____

_____

_____

The town was so filled with travelers that there was no place for Mary to give birth but in a place occupied by animals. The baby's first bed was a feeding trough. How does this fit in with Jesus's own words about himself in Luke 9:58?

_____

_____

_____

_____

_____

_____

With what John wrote in John 1:10–11?

_____

_____

_____

_____

_____

_____

_____

_____

With what Paul wrote later in Philippians 2:6–7?

_____

_____

_____

_____

_____

_____

_____

_____

6. Read Luke 2:8–20. Shepherding was a lowly occupation in Jesus's day. Shepherds were considered untrustworthy, and their work made them ceremonially unclean. Yet it was to these social outcasts that the good news first came. "Today in the town of David a Savior has been born to you" (v. 11).

Observe details:

What was the shepherds' initial reaction to the words of the angel?

_____

_____

_____

_____

_____

_____

What was the sign whereby they would recognize their Messiah?

_____

_____

_____

_____

_____

_____

After the multitude of angels had praised God, they left. What did the shepherds decide to do?

_____

_____

_____

_____

_____

How soon did they do it?

_____

_____

_____

_____

_____

What do you think their emotional response was when they found Mary and Joseph and the baby?

_____

_____

_____

_____

_____

What did they do as a result?

_____

_____

_____

_____

What was the reaction of those to whom they told their story?

_____

_____

_____

_____

_____

What was Mary's reaction to all that had happened?

_____

_____

_____

_____

_____

Mary reflected on these events, and so should we. It has been suggested that if the birth took place in winter, the shepherds may have been raising sheep for sacrifice at Passover a few months later. If this is so, what spiritual significance would this have to all believers (Exodus 12:21–22; John 1:29; 1 Corinthians 5:7; Hebrews 9:26).

_____

_____

_____

_____

What significance does it hold for you?

_____

_____

_____

_____

_____

_____

Mary not only pondered these events, she treasured them in her heart. How do you think she did this?

_____

_____

_____

_____

_____

_____

7. Read Luke 2:21–24. Eight days after Jesus's birth, Jesus was circumcised and officially named Jesus. Forty days after His birth, his parents presented Him to the Lord at the temple in Jerusalem. At this time they brought a pair of doves as an offering. The offering of birds instead of a lamb confirms that Jesus was born into a poor family. What impact does this truth have on your heart?

_____

_____

_____

_____

_____

_____

8. Read Luke 2:25–40 and note the providential timing as the Spirit brings Simeon and later Anna into the temple courts to meet up with Joseph, Mary, and Jesus. How does this confirm to your own heart that God is sovereign in all things? That even so-called little details are in His control?

_____

_____

_____

_____

Observe details:

Describe Simeon's attitude (vv. 28–29).

_____

_____

_____

_____

_____

_____

What had his eyes seen (v. 30)?

_____

_____

_____

_____

_____

_____

How does he describe it (v. 32)?

_____

_____

_____

_____

_____

_____

What was Joseph and Mary's response to Simeon's words (v. 33)?

_____

_____

_____

_____

_____

_____

_____

What personal message did he have for Mary (v. 34)?

_____

_____

_____

_____

_____

_____

What do we learn about Anna (vv. 36–37)?

_____

_____

_____

_____

_____

_____

What special message was she given to proclaim (v. 38)?

_____

_____

_____

_____

_____

_____

_____

_____

_____

_____

_____

_____

_____

_____

_____

A Closer Look at My Life

9. It has been said that Mary had a journaling heart. Although she probably didn't have access to writing materials, she did think things through with God. Putting yourself in Mary's sandals can help you do the same thing.

Imagine that night has fallen and the shepherds have come and gone. Except for Joseph and the baby, you are all alone. In your journal, write down your thoughts—what did you feel as you held your baby in your arms and when the shepherds worshiped? Treasure these moments in your heart.

Now shift the focus of your writing. Are there some things that have happened to you that you need to treasure in your heart? Some verses that God gave you at a crisis time in your life? How will you go about treasuring those things? Now, today? Next week? Write these in your journal.

10. You can do the same thing again by returning home with Mary after she and Joseph presented Jesus to God. Imagine that Simeon has held your baby in his arms and praised God with words you're not sure you understand. He blessed you but also told you about a sword that would pierce your heart. Then Anna came in. A woman of prayer, she gave thanks to God and then spoke of your Son being the redemption of Jerusalem. What did Simeon and Anna mean?

As you ponder these events with Mary, ask yourself these questions: Am I willing to trust my future into the hands of God and give Him thanks for all He's doing in my life? Am I willing to believe that what He had said, He will indeed do? Am I willing to trust Him with the pain of my past? My present? My future? Am I willing to spend time in His presence pondering His ways, His Word, and His heart?

Action Steps I Can Take Today

Choose one of the following activities:

11. Read several verses from this week's Scriptures and spend time meditating on them. Read them through several times, slowly and thoughtfully. Ask yourself questions. Ask God questions. Personalize what you're reading into a prayer and write it in your journal.

12. Reread Mary's song (Luke 1:46–55). How do you think the events Mary experienced in chapter 2 deepened her understanding of who God is? Write about this in your journal.

13. Choose a truth from Mary's song that expresses who God is and ask God to teach it to you through experience. Write in your journal about what you are learning and how you are experiencing Him. Make this an ongoing activity that you do weekly as you go through this study.

3

Mary, Jesus's Mother

A Woman Who Learned to Let Go

In lesson 1, we saw the intimate relationship that Mary as a young woman had cultivated with God. She knew Him as mighty, sovereign, her merciful Savior and deliverer. Because she knew Him, she trusted Him. She could even say to Gabriel, God's messenger, "I am the Lord's servant. . . . May it be to me as you have said" (Luke 1:38).

In lesson 2 we saw how Mary trusted God as she went about her daily tasks. Because she trusted Him, she faced the difficulties in her life with a quiet fortitude.

A stable for a birthplace? Lowly shepherds the first to visit her baby? Her own offering of two small doves in the temple? Not for her and Joseph the offering of the wealthy but the offering of the poor.

Mary's reaction to these things was to focus on the glory of God. She saw it in the worship of the shepherds. It was confirmed to her in the words of Simeon and Anna. So many things for Mary to ponder through with God—to treasure in her heart.

1. How does your own habit of thinking things through with God compare with Mary's?

_____

_____

_____

_____

_____

_____

Can you think of a time when you spent a lot of time talking to God about a particular situation? What did you learn as a result?

_____

_____

_____

_____

_____

A Closer Look at the Problem

Mary's habit of sharing her innermost thoughts with God reveals her to have been a godly woman. But she was far from a perfect human being. In this week's Scriptures we will see that Mary sometimes—not all the time, but sometimes—struggled with letting go of her preconceived ideas of what God would do. It wasn't always easy for her to accept His way as being absolutely perfect, especially when it was different from her way of doing things.

2. It's the same with us. It isn't always easy to . . .

- accept God's leading through our spiritual leaders rather than directly from God himself.
- let the ones we love most move out of our direct care.
- accept God's timing when it's a whole lot different from ours.
- realize that the people we love will sometimes do things that don't fit with what we think they should be doing.

Have you ever experienced difficulty in a situation similar to one of these? What happened?

_____

_____

_____

_____

_____

_____

_____

_____

_____

_____

_____

_____

_____

_____

_____

_____

A Closer Look at God's Truth

3. Read Matthew 2:1–12. A new star had risen in the east, and magi from a far country came to Jerusalem looking for the new king of the Jews. A disturbed King Herod heard these men were in the city and called together the teachers and temple officials to find out where the Messiah, the Christ, would be born. What Scripture did the teachers quote?

_____

_____

_____

_____

_____

_____

What did Herod do as a result of their report?

_____

_____

_____

_____

_____

What happened to the star?

_____

_____

_____

_____

_____

Remembering Mary's habit of thinking things through with God, what do you think might be her reaction to the visit of these magi (vv. 11–12)?

_____

_____

_____

_____

4. The story doesn't end here. That night Joseph had a dream. Read Matthew 2:13–23. Pay particular attention to verses 13–14 and 19–23. Whom had God put in charge of this little family?

_____

_____

_____

_____

_____

_____

Do you think that following Joseph's leadership was easy or difficult for Mary? Explain your answer.

_____

_____

_____

_____

_____

_____

Describe what happened during their time in Egypt.

_____

_____

_____

_____

_____

_____

After Herod's death, an angel appeared to Joseph in a dream. What did Joseph do?

_____

_____

_____

_____

_____

_____

_____

What did he do when he heard that Archelaus, Herod's son, a cruel tyrant, reigned in Judea?

_____

_____

_____

_____

_____

_____

How do you think Mary might have felt when he decided to return to their old hometown of Nazareth? Why might it have been easier for Mary to have gone somewhere else?

_____

_____

_____

_____

_____

_____

What can you learn from Mary's acceptance of Joseph's leading in the difficult and dangerous situations they encountered after leaving Bethlehem?

_____

_____

_____

_____

_____

_____

Home to Nazareth

Luke's Gospel describes the years that follow these events as a time when "the child grew and became strong; he was filled with wisdom, and the grace of God was upon him" (Luke 2:40).

In the godly home of Joseph and Mary in Nazareth, Jesus was taught the Scriptures. He learned obedience to His parents and to the law. At age twelve boys began preparing to take their places as sons of the covenant in the religious community the following year. This made it especially important that Jesus's family attend the Feast of the Passover. They did this by going together to Jerusalem in a great caravan.

At Jerusalem in the Father's House

Read Luke 2:41–46. After the feast, on the way back to Nazareth, Jesus turned up missing at the end of a day of travel. Since He was twelve years old, He might have been either with the women and children or with the men and older boys, if the families were grouped this way in the caravan. It is natural to assume that each parent supposed He was with the other.

Another day of travel would have been required for Joseph and Mary to make the trip back to Jerusalem. It wasn't until the third day that they found Him.

5. Read Luke 2:46–50. Describe the scene Mary and Joseph saw as they entered the temple courts.

_____

_____

_____

_____

_____

_____

What did they hear?

_____

_____

_____

_____

_____

What did they observe in the attitudes of the teachers of the law?

_____

_____

_____

_____

_____

_____

_____

_____

What words in the text describe Joseph and Mary's very human emotions?

_____

_____

_____

_____

_____

_____

What did Mary ask Jesus?

_____

_____

_____

_____

_____

_____

Jesus responded to Mary's questions by drawing a distinction between His parents and God, His true Father (v. 49). The questions He asked reveal that He knew His mission—He had to be about His father's business—and that His parents should have known. Why do you think Mary and Joseph didn't understand?

_____

_____

_____

_____

_____

6. Read Luke 2:51–52. Immediately after Jesus spoke of His divinity, He showed His perfect humanity (v. 51). How did He do that?

_____

_____

_____

_____

_____

_____

Compare Luke 2:51 with Luke 2:17-19. What do you think there is about these two situations that caused Mary to treasure them? To spend time pondering them? Write your thoughts in your journal.

A Wedding in Cana

The years slid by. Joseph was no longer with the family, and Jesus was rejected at Nazareth (Luke 4:16-31). When a wedding was celebrated at Cana, about nine miles north of his hometown, Jesus and His disciples were invited.

7. Read John 2:1–5 and observe what was happening. As you do, keep in mind that Mary, possibly a close relative of the couple, may have held some responsibility for the celebration. If so, she would have been deeply concerned for the bride and groom. In the closely knit communities of that day, failing to provide enough wine would have haunted the couple all their lives. Why did Mary express her concern to Jesus?

_____

_____

_____

_____

_____

_____

How did Jesus reply?

_____

_____

_____

_____

_____

How did Mary react to His words?

_____

_____

_____

_____

_____

_____

8. In spite of Jesus's words that the time was not yet right for Him, to make himself known to the world, He did something that had never been done before. Read John 2:6–11. What did He do?

_____

_____

_____

_____

_____

_____

Why do you think He did it?

_____

_____

_____

_____

_____

_____

What did His new disciples do as a result of His action that day?

_____

_____

_____

_____

_____

_____

Even though Jesus had to remind Mary of His mission on earth, there was beauty in her attitude. She accepted His independence and submission to His God-given task with grace, then quietly retired from the scene—after she instructed the servants to obey His every command.

Mary knew her Son's heart. Could she have known that this, His first miracle, would be a picture of His mission—water converted into wine, sinners converted into saints? We can only guess.

We do know that she was now willing to step aside and let Him do things God's way.

Near the Sea of Galilee

It seems that after the wedding in Cana, Mary and Jesus's brothers made their home in

Capernaum (John 2:12), while his sisters, probably married, stayed on in Nazareth. Although Mary and her other sons didn't usually accompany Jesus on His preaching tours, on one occasion they came to the edge of the crowd seeking Him.

9. Read Mark 3:20–21, 31–35. What was Mary and Jesus's brothers' purpose in going to where Jesus was at this time? What two things concerned them (vv. 20–21)?

_____

_____

_____

_____

_____

_____

What did Jesus's reply indicate to His family (vv. 33–34)?

_____

_____

_____

_____

_____

_____

To those who were listening to His words (vv. 33–34)?

_____

_____

_____

_____

_____

_____

To you, right now, where you are today?

_____

_____

_____

_____

_____

_____

A Closer Look at My Life

We have no record of how Mary and Jesus's brothers felt when Jesus asked who His mother and brothers were. We do know something about Mary, though. How might her past habit of thinking things through with God have served her at this time? How could the truth about those who did God's will being His family have stretched her heart and her understanding of who God is? How might it have brought her both sadness and joy?

_____

_____

_____

_____

_____

_____

Take a look at your own heart right now. Have you allowed Jesus to see the hurts buried there? The misunderstandings? Even past rejections that you might perceive as having come from God himself?

If you have accepted Jesus as your Savior, His words are for you. You are His family. You can trust Him, and because you can, you can stop trying to do everything in your own strength.

Action Steps I Can Take Today

10. Letting go of each one of the things you have buried inside your heart will free you to more fully share your life with God. In your jounal, make a list of people, situations, emotions, or anything else you are trying to control in your own strength. Underneath your list, write the words Mary addressed to the servants at the wedding feast (John 2:5).

11. Write Mary's words on a file card to carry with you this week. Refer to it often and jot down any steps of obedience you feel God is asking you to take. At the end of the week, share with one other person what you sense He is saying. Pray over it together. Ask God to give you the courage to do whatever you believe He is asking you to do.

4

Mary Magdalene and an Unnamed Woman

Women with Difficult Pasts

Today's lesson introduces us to another Mary—Mary Magdalene, one of the women who accompanied Jesus and His disciples on their preaching tours and cared for their needs.

Little is known about this Mary's past aside from Luke's first mention of her as having been delivered from seven demons (Luke 8). Some scholars think that the unnamed woman who anointed Jesus while He was at dinner in the home of Simon the Pharisee in the preceding chapter was Mary Magdalene. Others say, "No way."

No one can say positively one way or the other. However, a careful study of both women shows that they both had difficult pasts. This week's lesson will help us understand that no matter how much baggage we're carrying, when we understand forgiveness, there is a glorious freedom to love with the whole heart.

Release from the guilt of past sins enables us to express our love and gratitude to the one who forgave us. Jesus's words to the unnamed woman can be said of Mary Magdalene and of us, "She who is forgiven much, loves much."

A Closer Look at the Problem

The following note was given to me by a young woman I'll call Jan, after a teaching session.

> Tonight I heard you say that Jesus has power to not only forgive us from our sins but to free us to serve Him in newness of life. I wish I knew if that were really true. You see, I had sex with lots of men before I came to Jesus. He's forgiven me, I know, but every night the faces of those men drift past me in the darkness and I can't stop them.
>
> Sometimes I think of Mary Magdalene. She was tormented by seven demons and Jesus delivered her. I wonder, could she possibly have understood what I'm going through?
>
> My friends all tell me, though, that Mary Magdalene couldn't possibly have been a woman of the streets, that she was sort of like Peter. He was the leader of the disciples and Mary Magdalene was leader of the women who went with them on their preaching tours. They say Jesus would never have put someone who had been a prostitute in a position of leadership.
>
> What do you think? Is there a possibility that Mary Magdalene could have been the sinful woman who anointed Jesus's feet in the Pharisee's house? If she was, I think there might be hope for me.

I couldn't get Jan's note out of my thoughts. *Forgiveness. Are Jan's friends right? Are some sins more unforgivable than others?*

That night questions haunted me. I tossed and turned in my bed. *Mary Magdalene, who were you anyway? I know you were a tormented woman who was healed by the Master. That you later served Him by becoming one of the band of women who traveled with Him and His disciples. But were you also the prostitute whose joy at being forgiven overflowed in the perfume she lavished on Jesus?*

I found what I was searching for in God's Word. Whether the sinful woman and Mary Magdalene are the same woman or not, I do not know. But there are similarities between the two.

- Both women had difficult pasts.
- Both were forgiven much.
- Both loved much.
- Both served Jesus out of the overflow of that love.

Both the unnamed woman who anointed Jesus and Mary Magdalene experienced new beginnings and a new way of life. In Luke's Gospel the two are tied together with the parable Jesus told about the debtor and the debt.

A Closer Look at God's Truth

Read Luke 7:36–50. As you do, keep in mind that this account is not the same as the anointing mentioned in the other Gospels. Matthew, Mark, and John tell of an anointing by Mary, one of Jesus's devoted followers who lived in Bethany with her brother and sister. That took place at a dinner at the home of Simon the leper shortly before Jesus's death.

The anointing Luke records happened in Capernaum early in Jesus's ministry at the home of a Pharisee named Simon. A careful comparison of that account in Luke's Gospel with the others shows little similarity beyond the name of Simon (a common name in Palestine), the host.

The Sinner Who Came to Dinner

This unnamed woman took advantage of the social customs of the day that permitted needy people to visit such a banquet to receive the leftovers. Also, when a rabbi was invited to someone's house, others could stop by and listen to the conversation. It is not unusual, then, that this woman could slip into the room where the men were reclining at the table to eat, as was the custom of the day. What is unusual is that she was probably a well-known prostitute—Simon knew she was a "sinner" (v. 39)—and that she carried a small jar of perfume and was crying.

1. Describe what this woman did when she entered the room (vv. 37–38).

_____

_____

_____

_____

_____

_____

Why do you think she was weeping?

_____

_____

_____

_____

_____

_____

_____

How did her actions reveal her humility?

_____

_____

_____

_____

_____

_____

Her deep love?

_____

_____

_____

_____

_____

_____

2. What was Simon thinking about as he watched the woman (v. 39)?

_____

_____

_____

_____

_____

_____

What does Jesus's knowledge of Simon's thoughts tell you about who Jesus is (vv. 40–42)?

_____

_____

_____

_____

_____

_____

_____

_____

_____

A Parable Jesus Told

In the parable Jesus told next, one man was forgiven a debt ten times greater than another man's (one denarius was worth a day's wage). What question did Jesus ask Simon about His story (v. 42)?

_____

_____

_____

_____

_____

What was Simon's reply?

_____

_____

_____

_____

_____

Do you think Simon was surprised when Jesus applied the parable to the woman? Why or why not?

_____

_____

_____

_____

_____

Simon was a typical Pharisee. Sure of what the law demanded, he had no understanding of the love that transcends religious observances and religious regulations. He appears to have had much intellectual understanding but little heart understanding. Compare Simon's actions with those of the woman (vv. 44–47).

Simon's actions	The woman's actions
_____	_____
_____	_____
_____	_____
_____	_____
_____	_____
_____	_____

What do Simon's actions reveal about his heart?

_____

_____

_____

_____

_____

What do the woman's actions reveal about her heart?

_____

_____

_____

_____

_____

3. What do you learn about forgiveness from this parable and from Jesus's words (vv. 47–48)?

_____

_____

_____

_____

_____

An important point of the parable is that the woman's expression of love did not earn Jesus's forgiveness, although she expressed the devotion of one who already knew she had been forgiven (v. 47). What did Jesus say had saved her (v. 50)?

_____

_____

_____

_____

_____

_____

_____

Enter Mary Magdalene

The unnamed woman stepped into Luke's Gospel for a brief moment. Mary Magdalene follows. The same Jesus who showed mercy to the prostitute also showed mercy to Mary Magdalene.

4. Read Luke 8:1–3. This is the first mention made of Mary Magdalene. How is she described in this passage?

_____

_____

_____

_____

_____

_____

What were she and the other women doing?

_____

_____

_____

_____

_____

_____

More about Mary Magdalene

Mary was called by the name of her native city, Magdal, on the west bank of the Sea of Galilee. This ancient city was famous for dye works and fine woolen textures. Although trade, shipbuilding, fishing, fish curing, and agriculture brought great wealth to the city, its moral corruption was notorious.

Jesus of Galilee was ministering throughout Israel, and Mary Magdalene chose to follow Him and minister to His needs. She also chose to support Jesus and the Twelve from her own means.

5. Would you say that Mary Magdalene and the other women who were with Jesus and His disciples were truly liberated? Why or why not?

_____

_____

_____

_____

Luke refers to Mary Magdalene as an object of the grace and power of God in being released from seven demons. This strange reference to devils must mean that there was a mighty battle with evil for Mary's tortured soul.

6. Read Luke 8:26–39. These verses tell the story of man who had been controlled by demons. Read the account and note the contrast between his life before and after he met Jesus.

Before Jesus	After Jesus
_____	_____
_____	_____
_____	_____
_____	_____
_____	_____
_____	_____
_____	_____
_____	_____

Both the man from the region of the Gerasenes and Mary Magdalene were delivered by Jesus from their tortured pasts. What each was called to do afterward was different, however. The man who had once lived in the tombs now begged to go with Jesus.

7. Reread Luke 8:38–39. What did Jesus tell him to do?

_____

_____

_____

_____

_____

_____

Mary Magdalene, however, traveled with Jesus, caring for His needs. How do these two believers demonstrate the truth of Romans 12:6–8?

_____

_____

_____

_____

_____

_____

8. Read Philippians 1:6. What more do we learn about God's work in the life of a believer?

_____

_____

_____

_____

_____

_____

9. The Gospels give us other glimpses of the work God was doing in Mary Magdalene's life. Look up the following references and write down what you observe.

Matthew 27:55–56; Mark 15:40–41

_____

_____

_____

_____

_____

John 19:25–27

_____

_____

_____

_____

_____

Matthew 27:57–61; Luke 24:10

_____

_____

_____

_____

_____

_____

_____

John 20:1–18; Mark 16:9–10

_____

_____

_____

_____

_____

_____

Like the unnamed sinner, Mary Magdalene had not only been forgiven, she had been delivered from a tormented past. Her response to Jesus was an outflow of love. She gave Him everything she had—her money, her time, her entire life.

She who was forgiven much, loved much. She who loved much was given much. Mary Magdalene is always mentioned first when the women who followed Jesus are listed, which indicates she probably was their leader. To her also was given the privilege of being the first person to see Jesus after His resurrection. Joy filled her. "I have seen the Lord!" Jesus was alive! Mary ran to tell His disciples.

Released to Serve

Both women in this week's study loved Jesus with their whole hearts. Neither of them held anything back. Mary Magdalene's changed life expresses she has been both redeemed and forgiven. She serves with joy! No task was too large, no sacrifice too great to be made for the one who had forgiven them.

Both women knew their salvation was a gift. Totally undeserving, they had been saved by His grace. They were His "workmanship, created in Christ Jesus to do good works" (Ephesians 2:10).

10. How did these two woman demonstrate the truth of Ephesians 2:8–10?

_____

_____

_____

_____

_____

_____

_____

_____

_____

_____

A Closer Look at My Life

Take a look at your own heart. Have you been forgiven? Have you been released to serve your Lord? If not, what is holding you back?

Remember Jan? Completely overwhelmed by her past, she felt she had sinned so much she didn't have any idea how she could serve. But God had something better for her than a life of torment and empty regrets. Today Jan serves her Lord as a pastor's wife in a Midwestern town. She writes,

"The faces of the men are gone. I can't even remember their names. I think I'm a little bit like the sinner who anointed Jesus's feet, but I'm like Mary Magdalene too. My God has delivered me from the demons that tormented me. I'm teaching children, encouraging my husband, and caring for God's people. . . . My Lord has released me to serve Him in newness of life."

Action Steps I Can Take Today

11. The following steps will help you appropriate the forgiveness God has for you.

One. By faith, ask for forgiveness. Accept it as yours. Experiencing God's forgiveness can be a transforming moment in your relationship with your Lord. Express this revelation to your gracious Father in a prayer of praise for what He has done.

Two. Listen to God's Word. Find some verses that say He loves you, that He has forgiven you and accepted you, just the way you are. (Suggestion: Memorize Romans 8:1. Repeat it aloud each morning.)

Three. Draw near to God. The woman who anointed Jesus's feet wept at His feet. So did Mary Magdalene as she stood outside the empty tomb in the garden (John 20:11-13. What about you? Spend time in His presence today. Pour out your heart before Him. Thank Him for loving you just the way you are, with your weakness, your failures, your past with all its might-have-beens.

Four. Think on good things. Take an inventory of God's forgiveness to you. How has He shown you mercy? Compassion? Micah 7:19 and Psalm 103:12 are good verses to think on! God does not dwell upon our sins, and neither should we.

12. Evaluate your talents, your desires, and your resources. Taking all these into consideration, what work do you think God has planned for you to do? Write about it in your journal, then share it with a trusted friend and pray together.

Mary of Bethany

A Woman Who Desired to Be with Jesus

This week's study takes us to Bethany, a village located on the eastern slope of Mount Olivet, about two miles from Jerusalem. Here we meet Mary, the sister of Lazarus and Martha, for the first time. A woman with a quiet and gentle spirit, Mary of Bethany takes the role of a disciple by sitting at the feet of Jesus and listening to His words.

It was unusual for a woman in first-century Judaism to be accepted as a disciple by a teacher. However, because she had, she had an understanding of Jesus that surpassed that of the men. In a sense, she was a "support group of one" because she understood the meaning of Jesus's mission to earth. She knew He faced the cross.

The goal of this study is to see the reality of the cross and the power of the resurrection as Mary of Bethany saw them. She believed that Jesus was the Messiah, the Son of God, and that He was worthy of her worship. Her act of anointing Him before His death was a memorial of love poured out on her Lord.

A Closer Look at the Problem

Many Christians long to obey God's Word, pray without ceasing, and experience the joy of worship and service. Instead, the baby cries all day and sometimes, it seems, all night too. The lawn grows moss and has more bare spaces than it used to. The car payment is overdue; the garbage can overflows, and the phone keeps ringing.

Roberta, a woman with four almost-grown children, cried out, "Nothing is the way I thought it would be. Nothing! Don hates his job. He comes home depressed and angry. I get up at four in the morning and work in a warehouse all day. We seldom have meals together anymore. It's a sandwich on the run, a quick 'Got a game, Mom. See you later.' I never have time for myself—much less time for God. I've lost something that I once treasured and loved, and I don't know how to find it. I need to get back to my Lord, but there's no time, and I'm so tired."

Most of us can identify with Roberta. Can we really get to know God and worship Him with our whole hearts when confusion muddies our thoughts and everything seems to fall apart? Is discovering joy in the presence of our Lord really possible in spite of the sheer pain of existence in a crazy world?

Yes. But real worship can only come as we learn to sit at the feet of Jesus, listening to His words. That's what Mary of Bethany did.

A Closer Look at God's Truth

Our First Glimpse of Mary of Bethany

1. Read Luke 10:38–42. Picture the scene as you read these verses. Describe what you see.

_____

_____

_____

_____

_____

_____

What do you smell and hear?

_____

_____

_____

_____

_____

How would you describe the atmosphere of the house?

_____

_____

_____

_____

_____

What positive personality traits do you see in the sisters?
Martha (v. 38)

_____

_____

_____

_____

_____

Mary (v. 39)

_____

_____

_____

_____

_____

_____

Commentators suggest that this home in Bethany was one where Jesus often went. In this account Martha had invited Him into her home, but it was Mary who sat at His feet with a hungry heart.

We learn something of Martha's attitude when we recognize that "distracted" and "worried and upset" in verses 40–41 are from a Greek word meaning "to seek to promote oneself." When Martha complained about Mary not helping her, Jesus showed concern for Martha's anxiety but commended Mary for having her priorities in order.

Service begins at Jesus's feet.

The Sisters See Jesus's Resurrection Power

2. Read John 11:1–44. What kind of relationship do you sense this family has with Jesus by the message the sisters sent to Jesus (v. 3)?

_____

_____

_____

_____

_____

_____

How did Jesus respond to their message (v. 6)?

_____

_____

_____

_____

_____

_____

Jesus's close relationship with this family is evidenced by the way the sisters sent Him word that their brother was sick. They didn't demand that He come; their trust was evidenced in their simple appeal (v. 3). Yet when Jesus received their message, He didn't come. He stayed where He was two more days, explaining to His disciples that Lazarus's death was for God's glory. Meanwhile the sisters waited.

3. How long had Lazarus been in the tomb by the time Jesus arrived (v. 17)?

_____

_____

_____

_____

_____

_____

What did Martha do when she heard He was coming from Jerusalem to Bethany (v. 20)?

_____

_____

_____

_____

_____

_____

What did she say to Him? (v. 21)?

_____

_____

_____

_____

_____

By what claim did Jesus express His power (v. 25)?

_____

_____

_____

_____

_____

_____

Who did Martha say she believed Jesus to be (v. 27)?

_____

_____

_____

_____

_____

_____

4. How do you think Mary felt as she sat waiting in the house for Jesus (v. 20)?

_____

_____

_____

_____

_____

_____

Have you ever felt hurt or had deep needs, yet Jesus seemed far away or didn't seem to respond, at least not the way you wanted Him to? Enter into Mary's hurt by writing an entry she might have written in her journal while she waited.

_____

_____

_____

_____

_____

5. What was Mary's response when Martha told her Jesus was asking for her (vv. 28–33)?

_____

_____

_____

_____

_____

_____

What was Jesus's response to Mary's tears (vv. 33–35)?

_____

_____

_____

_____

_____

_____

Jesus was also deeply moved when He came to the tomb. Death is a close companion of sin and sorrow, but God is greater than the curse Satan brought into the world. Jesus looked up to heaven and spoke to His Father, then called out, "Lazarus, come out!"

6. Write a journal entry Mary might have written after Jesus raised her brother Lazarus from the dead. Express her wonder and joy (vv. 38–44).

_____

_____

_____

_____

_____

_____

Mary Worships at Jesus's Feet

7. We see Mary six weeks later in Bethany, at a dinner at the house of Simon the leper. Compare the three Scripture portions that tell about this incident. Write down your observations.

Matthew 26:6–13

_____

_____

_____

_____

_____

_____

_____

_____

_____

Mark 14:3–9

_____

_____

_____

_____

_____

_____

John 12:1–9

_____

_____

_____

_____

_____

_____

8. Compare the texts by asking questions. What details does John give that the others do not?

_____

_____

_____

_____

_____

_____

Which two Gospels say her act would be a special memorial of the gospel?

_____

_____

_____

_____

_____

_____

_____

_____

Which one says it was done in preparation for His burial?

_____

_____

_____

_____

_____

_____

Jesus comes to Mary's defense in all three Gospel accounts. How do you think this made Mary feel?

_____

_____

_____

_____

_____

_____

Whom do you identify with the most—the practical men or Mary in her lavish use of the nard? Explain your answer.

_____

_____

_____

_____

_____

_____

To worship means to respond to God. Mary responded to Jesus's love by giving what she had. Jesus put it into words in Mark 14:8: "She did what she could. She poured perfume on my body beforehand to prepare for my burial."

Mary's sacrifice was symbolized in the pouring out of her most valued possession. Her life and love is symbolized by the fragrance poured out on her Lord. Mary gave all. She worshiped at His feet.

A Closer Look at My Life

In each of these accounts, an ordinary house is filled with a fragrant aroma as Mary broke the jar of nard and poured the perfume on her Lord's head and feet. Keep in mind that this fragrance was often used for anointing the dead because its aroma was powerful enough to cover the scent of death. Some historians believe the fragrance could have followed Christ to the cross. Our Lord whose very robes had been perfumed by the fragrances of heaven (Psalm 45:7–8) was anointed by a woman in an act of adoration and worship.

Not only did her unselfish act of worship bring joy to the heart of her Master, this single act brought blessing to the entire world. But perhaps the greatest blessing of all is what Mary's gift of fragrance did for her Savior, teacher, and Lord.

This act took place before He went to the cross. Her love—expressed in perfume from a broken jar—followed Jesus to the upper room and the garden of Gethsemane. The aroma went with Him to the trial and then to the cross. When the disciples ran away or stayed at a distance, Mary's perfume lingered, perhaps reminding Jesus that her heart belonged to Him. Unseen, its fragrance would permeate His darkness and pain and reassure Him of her love and support.

Supreme love and sacrifice are shown in this single act. Once Mary's jar was broken, she could never again hug it to herself. The contents could never be put back.

Mary's life was a fragrance poured out. She demonstrated the glow of a life poured out in the sacrifice of her most valued possession as she gave her all to her Lord—with love.

But there's more. Just as the sweet perfume could have lingered on Jesus, so did it linger on the hands of Mary. The motif of fragrance is used throughout scripture. Paul wrote in 2 Corinthians 2:14–15, "But thanks be to God, who always leads us in triumphal procession in Christ and through us spreads everywhere the fragrance of the knowledge of him. For we are to God the aroma of Christ among those who are being saved and those who are perishing."

The woman who spends time each day listening to God's Word, the woman who worships and then places everything she has at the feet of Jesus, brings a spiritual fragrance to life, indefinable, perhaps even mysterious, so that ordinary places become fragrant with the presence of Christ.

Roses are grown for the Vienna market in great profusion and with much distillation of fragrance in a certain valley. If you were to visit at the time of the rose crop, wherever you would go for the rest of the day, the fragrance you would carry with you would betray where you had been.

The same is true of believers. When we spend time at the feet of the one who is altogether lovely, we too will carry a fragrance—a spiritual fragrance.

9. Some famous personalities have had fragrances named after them. Name a few. What are the connotations of some of them? What lies behind the lives of those they represent? Purity? Impurity? Holiness? Ungodliness?

_____

_____

_____

_____

_____

_____

Think about your life. If you had a fragrance named after you, what would it be? What would it represent?

_____

_____

_____

_____

_____

_____

How would it reflect your relationship with God?

_____

_____

_____

_____

_____

_____

10. As we spend time with Jesus, He purifies us. His righteousness produces character qualities within us that carry a distinct fragrance. Pick out the scent that came to your mind as you thought through the previous questions about the kind of fragrance you would like your life to have. Write several descriptive sentences about your choice, then explain why you chose that particular scent.

_____

_____

_____

_____

_____

Action Steps I Can Take Today

11. Mary worshiped Jesus for who He was. She saw Him as Isaiah saw Him. Meditate on Isaiah 9:6: "For to us a child is born, to us a son is given, and the government will be on his shoulders. And he will be called Wonderful Counselor [Mary sat at His feet and listened], Mighty God [she saw Him raise her brother from the dead], Everlasting Father [as a child trusts his father to meet his or her needs, so she trusted Jesus to come when she needed Him], Prince of Peace [He was the ruler of her life, the one worthy of her worship. Her peace grew as she recognized Jesus's power over the grave].

How do you need to see Jesus today? As your Wonderful Counselor? Your Mighty God? Everlasting Father? Prince of Peace? Choose the name you need most right now. Write it on a card and review it each morning as you address your prayer and your need for the day to the one with that name.

12. Jesus prophesied that wherever Mary's name would be mentioned, her act of devotion would be spoken of as a memorial to her. Describe Mary's act of worship by creating an acrostic. Working in your journal, follow the pattern given and add a descriptive word or phrase that begins with each letter. Then do one with the name of a family member or friend and the place where she lives. Use words and phrases that are descriptive of that person. Present your acrostic to the person you selected as a gift of your love.

M

A

R

Y

O

F

B

E

T

H

A

N

Y

At the Cross

Women Who Wept

Our study on the three Marys as role models for today's woman has taught us much about the women who walked with the Savior when He was here on earth. We've discovered truth about who God is, and we've seen His power—Jesus is the almighty Son of God.

Each of the women—Mary, Jesus's mother; Mary Magdalene and an unnamed woman; and Mary of Bethany—held a unique place in Jesus's life and ministry.

Jesus's mother Mary, chosen by God to raise His Son to manhood, is a woman of courage who chose to obey God, even when she didn't completely understand what that obedience would entail. From her we learned about trust, thinking things through with God, and letting go of our own agenda.

From Mary Magdalene and the woman who had been a prostitute, we saw the reality of forgiveness and love in action. Mary Magdalene was also a part of Jesus's itinerant ministry, a leader of the women who helped support Him financially and accompanied Him and His disciples on their preaching tours.

Mary of Bethany had the rare privilege of sitting at His feet as a disciple and later anointing Jesus's head and feet before the cross. She alone of His followers understood that He would die. Jesus said of her, "She has done what she could; she has anointed My body beforehand for the burial" (Mark 14:8 NASB).

This week's lesson takes us to the cross and the tomb. Both Jesus's mother and Mary Magdalene followed Jesus there. From a distance they, with other women, watched Joseph and Nicodemus prepare his body for burial. Then they slipped away.

The goal of this lesson is to see Jesus as they saw Him, to experience something of the agony they experienced as they watched the one they loved most of all die for their sins and the sins of the world.

And that isn't all. These women, although powerless to ease Jesus's suffering, still yearned to reach out, to minister to Him in whatever way they could.

A Closer Look at the Problem

Women want to help others. When someone dies or experiences a crisis or tragedy, we want to do something. We prepare and deliver meals when a young mother struggles with cancer. We gather gifts of food and clothing to give to families when fathers are unemployed.

A night out for single moms. Cookies for soldiers overseas. A quilt for the homeless. The list goes on and on. Women helping their families, friends, neighbors, and church family. Women doing what they can to help those less fortunate.

1. What are some of the things you've observed women doing for others?

_____

_____

_____

_____

_____

_____

Can you tell about a particular incident of service that impacted you personally? What effect did that particular ministry have on your life or on the life of someone you love?

_____

_____

_____

_____

_____

_____

The women in Jesus's life had servant hearts. They are seen with Jesus and the twelve in Luke 8:1–3 when Jesus went about to cities and villages. They stood at the cross as close as the soldiers would allow. After He was dead, they still sought to do something, even when the only thing left for them to do was prepare spices for anointing His dead body.

These women inspired me by their raw courage and willingness to be there for the Lord they loved. Let's follow them now as they take the way of the cross.

A Closer Look at God's Truth

Careful observation of each of the Gospel accounts give us glimpses of the women at the cross and the tomb. But what about Mary of Bethany. Where was she?

Some have considered the question of Mary of Bethany's whereabouts, but the answer is not found in Scripture. If she was at the cross, she is not named.

Someone has suggested that Mary and her family may have had to leave Bethany because of their close involvement with Jesus when He raised Lazarus from the dead and His arrest shortly after. We don't know, but we do know that Mary was an eyewitness of her brother Lazarus's resurrection. Could she have chosen not to go to the tomb because she knew that Jesus wouldn't be there? We can only wonder.

Observing the Text

Developing good observation skills is important for Bible study. Sometimes we come to a passage of Scripture and, because we've read it often, we fail to look closely at what is actually there.

One way to overcome this is to imagine we're looking at the passage from the perspective of someone else. We're going to do that now as we look at the four Gospel accounts of the cross and the tomb from the perspective of the women who followed Jesus.

As you read each of the Scripture portions in question 2, try to imagine what either Jesus's mother or Mary Magdalene experienced that long-ago day. Where was she going? Who was with her? What did she see and hear? How did she act? What did she feel? Purposefully stepping out of your own perspective will help you see things you might otherwise miss.

Reminder: becoming a careful observer of the Word of God takes practice—and time. Asking who, what, when, where, why, and how questions will slow you down and help you see what is happening. It can also help you ponder the scene more carefully.

2. Now choose either Jesus's mother or Mary Magdalene as your viewpoint woman and write down fifteen or twenty observations for each Scripture portion below from her perspective. (You might want to use your journal so you'll have plenty of space to record what your character experienced.)
Matthew 27: 32–56

_____

_____

_____

_____

_____

Mark 15:21–41

_____
_____
_____
_____
_____

Luke 23:26–49

_____
_____
_____
_____
_____
_____

John 19:17–37

_____
_____
_____
_____
_____

Putting the Accounts Together

3. Luke is the only writer who mentions in detail the women of Jerusalem who followed Jesus and Simon who carried His cross. What did these women do (Luke 23:27)?

_____
_____
_____
_____
_____
_____
_____
_____

How does Jesus respond to their cries (vv. 28–31)?

_____

_____

_____

_____

_____

_____

What does this show you about Jesus's compassion for women and children?

_____

_____

_____

_____

_____

_____

4. Read John 19:25–27. John included an incident that none of the other writers mention. What emotions do you think Jesus's mother felt as He looked at her and called her "Dear woman"?

_____

_____

_____

_____

_____

As He gave her into the care of the disciple He was closest to?

_____

_____

_____

_____

_____

_____

_____

_____

How does this incident fit in with what Simon said to Mary at Jesus's presentation at the temple in Jerusalem when He was a baby (Luke 2:35)?

_____

_____

_____

_____

_____

_____

_____

_____

What insight does it give you into the heart of Jesus's mother as she stood close to the cross?

_____

_____

_____

_____

_____

5. At noon, a deep heavy darkness fell over the crucifixion scene. Three of the Gospels record it (Matthew 27:45; Mark 15:33; Luke 23:44–45). What do you suppose Jesus's mother thought and felt when this intense darkness fell upon everyone?

_____

_____

_____

_____

_____

What about Mary Magdalene? What do you think she felt?

_____

_____

_____

_____

For three hours Jesus endured the pain and darkness alone. When He finally did cry out, what did He say (Matthew 27:46)?

_____

_____

_____

_____

_____

_____

Jesus, for the first time in eternity, had been forsaken by the Father; the heavenly Father had caused the sins of all mankind to be dumped on His Son's shoulders (Isaiah 53:6; Galatians 3:13). Do you think Mary Magdalene understood what was happening?

And what about His mother? We do know that Mary, from the beginning, knew who Jesus was. Whether she had grasped the impact the death of her Son would have on the whole world, both then and in the future, is not known. But she knew she loved and believed in Him.

6. What about believers today? Do we see the bigger picture more clearly now than these women of long ago?

_____

_____

_____

_____

_____

_____

_____

_____

Not only did Jesus endure the darkness, He endured great thirst as well. He who was the water of life (John 4:14; 7:37–38; Isaiah 55:1–3), who freely gave to all who were thirsty and came to Him, now said, "I am thirsty" (John 19:28). After He received the sponge that was lifted to his lips, He cried out with a loud voice, "It is finished!" (Matthew 27:50; Luke 23:46; John 19:30). Then He yielded up His spirit. Jesus had accomplished His mission on earth. It was a glorious victory!

7. Read Matthew 27:57–61; Mark 15:42–47; Luke 23:50–55; John 19:38–42. John is the only Gospel writer who doesn't mention that the women watched as Jesus's body was prepared for burial and placed in the tomb. He does, however, give information not mentioned by the others. What is this information?

_____

_____

_____

_____

_____

_____

_____

_____

_____

Taking John's information into account, describe what the women saw as they watched.

_____

_____

_____

_____

_____

_____

What did they decide to do (Luke 23:55–56)?

_____

_____

_____

_____

_____

_____

_____

_____

_____

A Closer Look at My Life

8. Go back over these Scriptural accounts and find the incident in the crucifixion that most touched you. Describe it in your own words, then explain why it moved you.

_____

_____

_____

_____

_____

_____

How do you think it affected the heart of the woman you chose to walk with as you followed Jesus's steps to the cross in question 2?

_____

_____

_____

_____

_____

_____

9. The women who followed Jesus to Golgotha were powerless to do anything to help their Lord. They couldn't keep the crowd from their jeering mockery or stop the soldiers from pounding in the nails. The only thing they could do was be there. Have you—or are you now—in a situation where there is nothing you can do except pray and be there for someone? Tell about it.

_____

_____

_____

_____

_____

What did you learn or what are you learning from this experience?

_____

_____

_____

_____

What more do you feel you need to learn?

_____

_____

_____

_____

_____

_____

Action Steps I Can Take Today

10. Seeing Jesus's love and suffering up close and personal does things to one's heart. Write a letter to Jesus. Let Him know how you felt as you followed Him to the cross. Thank Him for the faithful women who went with you. Ask Him to help you become as faithful as they were. Read your letter aloud to Jesus as your love gift to Him.

11. Joseph and Nicodemus weren't alone as they anointed Jesus's body and wrapped Him in linen cloths. The women watched—there was nothing left for them to do except go home and prepare their spices. With their own hands they would anoint the one they loved.

Small things perhaps? Not so. An act of love never escapes the eye of the heavenly Father. Read Matthew 10:42; 25:37–40. What act of kindness is Jesus asking you to do today, or soon? Write a note to your child's teacher? Put a hand on a friend's shoulder? Spend an hour in chitchat with an elderly parent or neighbor?

12. Tell a friend about the action you feel the Holy Spirit is asking you to take. Then pray together. Ask your friend to hold you accountable as you follow through in obedience to your Lord.

At the Empty Tomb

Women Who Rejoiced

Six o'clock. The Jewish Sabbath had begun.

The disciples had scattered. Jesus's mother was at John's home. Mary Magdalene and her friend, another Mary, had left the garden with heavy hearts. Jesus was dead.

Not only did Roman soldiers watch over the tomb, Pilate had ordered that it be sealed with a Roman seal. A cord covered with clay or wax was tied to the stone and the official seal impressed into it.

It was over. Jesus's body had been sealed in a cavern of darkness.

A Closer Look at the Problem

But wait—the greatest miracle in all history is about to be enacted! It had begun in heaven.

Sometime before the women arrived at the tomb with their spices on the day after the Sabbath, an angel descended. Could it be that the impact of the angel's feet as they hit the ground caused the earth to quake?

1. Read Matthew 28:2–4 and write down your observations of this awesome event. *The NIV Study Bible* **says that "although Matthew speaks of one angel (not two, Mt 28:2) and Mark of a young man in white (Mk 16:5), this is not strange because frequently only the spokesman is noted and an accompanying figure is not mentioned."[1]**

_____

_____

_____

_____

_____

_____

Have you ever experienced an earthquake? If so, describe what happened and your reaction to it.

_____

_____

_____

_____

_____

How does your earthquake compare to the one in Matthew 28?

_____

_____

_____

_____

_____

_____

A Tomb in a Garden

Even though the women had experienced the earthquake, they were unprepared for the open tomb. Let's try to determine what happened next by first looking back at the events that preceded their arrival in the garden.

Although John had taken Mary to his home, Mary Magdalene and the other Mary had stayed at the cross until Christ's death. Reluctant to leave, they lingered, watching as loving hands took Jesus down from the cross and carried Him to the freshly hewed tomb.

The women followed (Luke 23:54–56; John 19:38–42).

The Jewish custom was to bathe the body, then wrap it in fine linen; the head was wrapped with a separate piece of cloth. Nicodemus brought a mixture of myrrh and aloes, which the men placed in the folds of linen. They had to hurry; the beginning of the Sabbath was almost upon them.

The watching women saw it all. They observed the heavy rock, much like a millstone, that the men pushed into the deep groove outside the entrance.

The hour heralding the Sabbath was nearer now; the Jewish law forbade devout Jews to either work or travel. The women had to hurry home.

But they would return.

2. What do you think the women talked about as they scurried to their homes?

_____

_____

_____

_____

_____

_____

_____

_____

_____

_____

_____

_____

_____

_____

_____

_____

_____

_____

_____

A Closer Look at God's Truth

Mary Magdalene had witnessed many miracles as she traveled with Jesus and His followers. But she hadn't expected the awful events that led to the crucifixion, or the death and
burial of her beloved Lord. Nevertheless, she had been there to support her Master.

Only a woman who loved like this would have come to the garden on the first day of
the week before the sun had risen. Filled with love and appreciation for the one who had
delivered her from the bondage of seven demons and brought her into new freedom, she
hurried to the tomb.

3. Read John 20:1–2. What did Mary Magdalene first observe?

_____

_____

_____

_____

_____

_____

What did she do?

_____

_____

_____

_____

_____

_____

What did she say?

_____

_____

_____

_____

_____

_____

Piecing Together the Details

It is hard to put together the pieces of the details of the events that took place that long-ago
morning. The women could have arrived at the tomb at two different times, or they could

have taken different paths to get there. Exactly how it happened, we don't know. But we do know that Mary Magdalene had left before dawn to go to the tomb (Matthew 28:1).

When she arrived, the soldiers were gone and the angel was no longer sitting on the stone. Mary's immediate reaction was to run back to Jerusalem. In a panic of confusion, she ran to tell Peter and John that the body was gone (John 20:2).

4. Who did Mary think had taken away the Lord?

_____

_____

_____

_____

_____

_____

What were her fears about Christ's body?

_____

_____

_____

_____

_____

5. What happened next? Read John 20:3–10. What did Peter observe when he looked inside the tomb?

_____

_____

_____

_____

_____

What do Peter's observations say to your heart about the reality of the resurrection?

_____

_____

_____

_____

The two disciples soon left the tomb. The quiet evidence of the empty grave clothes, the strips of linen cloth, had convinced John that Jesus was alive. What do you think he told Mary, Jesus's mother, when he returned home?

_____

_____

_____

_____

_____

_____

Alone in the Garden

And what of Mary Magdalene? Where is she?

Mary had returned to the tomb. Peter and John were gone now, but something deep inside Mary compelled her to be there to mourn for her Lord.

Perhaps she hoped to find Peter and John still there, but they weren't. There was no one there with whom she might share her grief and dismay over the missing body. She was alone.

Pain ripped through her. She began to weep and sob. And then—

6. Read John 20:11–18. What does Mary Magdalene see and hear?

_____

_____

_____

_____

_____

How did she respond?

_____

_____

_____

_____

_____

_____

_____

_____

What did she do next?

_____

_____

_____

_____

_____

_____

Who did she think Jesus was?

_____

_____

_____

_____

_____

Why do you think she didn't recognize Him?

_____

_____

_____

_____

_____

When Jesus spoke her name, in an instant Mary went from extreme grief to great joy. She cried out, "Rabboni!" which means " Teacher" What else did she do?

_____

_____

_____

_____

_____

_____

_____

_____

What do you think Jesus meant when He told Mary, "Do not hold on to me, for I have not yet returned to the Father"?

_____

_____

_____

_____

_____

_____

Could it be that Mary thought Jesus was returning to heaven to continue the ministry He had before He came to earth? Or was He actually saying, "Please don't cling to me, for I shall soon be ascending to heaven, and there is much for me to do in this short period before I leave."
What did Jesus ask Mary Magdalene to do?

_____

_____

_____

_____

_____

Why do you think He used the pronouns *my* and *your* when He spoke of His Father and His God to Mary?

_____

_____

_____

_____

_____

Jesus was alive! What effect did this news have on Mary Magdalene as she hurried to tell the disciples? What were the first words she said to His disciples (v. 18)?

_____

_____

_____

_____

A Closer Look at My Life

Mary Magdalene spoke words that have power to make the senses sing: "I have seen the Lord!" It was the message Jesus gave her to give to the disciples. It was the message of the empty tomb.

A Time to Ponder

Did Mary's heart form new words to the psalms the Israelites sang in their worship at the temple? Could she have sung them aloud as she ran through the garden that long-ago Sunday morning?

We don't know. The Scriptures in the following scenes[1] are paraphrased from Psalm 29:1–9; 1 Chronicles 16:32–33; Psalm 30:2–5, 11–12. We can only imagine how Mary's joy might have spiraled upward into the heavens:

> Ascribe to the LORD, O mighty ones, ascribe to the LORD glory and strength. Ascribe to the LORD the glory due his name; worship the LORD in the splendor of his holiness.
>
> Let the sea resound, and all that is in it; let the fields be jubilant, and everything in them! Then the trees of the forest will sing, they will sing for joy before the LORD.

Mary Magdalene had been present at Calvary. She experienced the darkness, felt the earthquake. She had witnessed her Lord's dying glory. Perhaps her heart rang with words like these:

> The voice of my Savior and the voice of my Father are one. The voice of the LORD is over the garden. The God of glory thunders; the LORD thunders over Mount Calvary. The voice of the LORD is powerful; the voice of the LORD breaks the olive trees. The LORD breaks in pieces the chains of death. He makes the hills around Jerusalem skip like calves and Mount Calvary like a young wild ox. The voice of the LORD strikes with flashes of lightning. The voice of the LORD shakes Jerusalem. The LORD shakes the gates of the city. The voice of the LORD twists the oaks and strips the forest bare. The voice of the LORD speaks my name.
>
> O LORD my God, I called to you for help, and you came. You healed my broken heart; you made me sing.

---

1. From *Created to Worship*, published by David C Cook / Accent Publications. Copyright 1991 Eva Gibson, Norman Jewell. Publisher permission required to reproduce. All rights reserved.

Mary's feet must have skipped, exultation bursting from her as she ran to tell the others.

> You brought Jesus up from the grave. You spared me from going down into
> the pit. You went there so I wouldn't have to!
>
> Sing to the LORD, O brethren of His; praise His holy name. For the
> Father's anger lasts only a moment, that moment as darkness fell. But
> His favor lasts a lifetime. Weeping remains for a night, rejoicing comes
> in the dawn.

She might have stopped in the middle of the path and spread her arms wide, the sun falling on her face as she continued her song:

> At sunrise you came to me! You turned my wailing into dancing; you
> removed my sackcloth and clothed me with joy, that my heart may sing
> to you and not be silent. O LORD my God, I will give you thanks forever.

Even though we cannot know what was in Mary's heart as she ran to tell the disciples that Jesus was risen, we can see Calvary and the resurrection foreshadowed in Old Testament Scriptures. We can experience the joy of God's Word.

Songs in Scripture can become our songs.

A Heavenly Encounter

Mary wasn't the only woman who was entrusted with the message that Christ was risen. Jesus also appeared to a whole group of women.

7. Read Matthew 28:5–8; Luke 24:1–8. What did these women discover as they entered the tomb?

_____

_____

_____

_____

_____

_____

The message the angel gave the women was one of great hope. What did he say?

_____

_____

_____

_____

An Even Greater Encounter

8. Read Matthew 28:9–10. What emotions did the women express in these verses?

_____

_____

_____

_____

_____

_____

What did they do when they came face-to-face with their risen Lord?

_____

_____

_____

_____

_____

_____

9. Meditate on the power of the resurrection. The power of the message to "go and tell" that was given to Mary Magdalene and the other women is the same message we have been given to tell the world.

Ponder this great truth. Then ask the Holy Spirit to empower you to tell your world—your family, community, the people you work with—the good news of Jesus's death and resurrection.

Action Steps I Can Take Today

10. Mary's song in this lesson's "A Closer Look at My Life" section is based on a selection of verses that are descriptive of the joy she felt as she ran to tell the disciples the good news. Choose verses and phrases to match a song in your own heart. Or select verses and phrases that express a song you wish you had in your heart. Either way, read, sing, or write the words in your journal. Read or sing them back to your Lord.

11. Read Mark 16:9–11; Luke 24:9–11. Even though the men didn't believe the words of the women, the women knew what they had seen and heard. Jesus had risen, and they were sent to tell His disciples. Jesus himself would vindicate their story.

Jesus will vindicate your story too. When is the last time you told someone about the death and resurrection of Jesus? Whom will you tell today? This week?

12. A prayer for you to pray. *Lord Jesus, You have given me a song to sing! Now give me the courage to sing it, whether it be in words, actions, or attitude, to those I come in contact today. Let my life and lips proclaim that you have risen indeed! I love you, worship you, praise you with my whole heart. You are my Lord and my God.*

8

In the Upper Room

Women Who Waited

In lesson 7, we watched the faithful women who followed Jesus to the cross return to the tomb. Their arms laden with spices, they were prepared to do what they could for the one they loved.

But instead of a dead body wrapped in grave clothes, they discovered an empty tomb and a risen Savior. Mary Magdalene's announcement to the disciples, "I have seen the Lord!" echoes in our hearts.

In the forty days between Jesus's resurrection and His return to heaven, Jesus made ten appearances. The wonder of these experiences must have been written deep on the hearts and minds of those who loved Him. During this time some of them talked with Him as He appeared out of nowhere and disappeared again. They ate with Him and touched His hands. The wonder of it all is beyond our comprehension.

At the end of the forty days, Jesus appeared to His disciples in Jerusalem. There He instructed them to "stay in the city until you have been clothed with power from on high" (Luke 24:49). They heard His words and believed His promise: "You will receive power when the Holy Spirit comes on you; and you will be my witnesses in Jerusalem, and in all Judea and Samaria, and to the ends of the earth" (Acts 1:8).

From there He led them out to Bethany, where He gave His final farewell: "He lifted up his hands and blessed them" (Luke 24:50). His gesture of blessing was what the Jewish high priest would do after finishing the sacrifice for sin (Leviticus 9:22-24).

While He was blessing His disciples, Jesus began to rise into the air. From the Mount of Olives, He passed into the clouds.

Were the women who loved Him with the disciples who watched Him ascend to heaven? In this, our final lesson, we take our last look at these women as they waited in the upper room for His promise. Our goal: to discover practical insights about how we can wait expectantly, patiently, and productively.

A Closer Look at the Problem

Jesus had instructed His followers to "stay in Jerusalem and wait."

Wait? But waiting is hard. Even though the Word of God says, "Be still before the LORD and wait patiently for him" (Psalm 37:7), waiting isn't easy. In fact most of us, if we're honest, will admit we don't like to wait. We might even feel faint resentment that God would suggest that waiting is a part of His plan for us.

Consider this from a prophet who learned to wait: "But as for me, I watch in hope for the LORD, I wait for God my Savior; my God will hear me" (Micah 7:7).

Watch—hope—wait. When your best friend has been diagnosed with cancer and faces months of chemotherapy—then surgery?

Watch—hope—wait. When your marriage is falling apart and you face your own failure and inadequacies? Can God really bring beauty out of your broken pieces?

Watch—hope—wait. When you have to move for the fourth time in a year? When the children show signs of insecurity and loss? When we find ourselves crying out, "Lord, how long do we have to wait?" "Since ancient times no one has heard, no ear has perceived, no eye has seen any God besides you, who acts on behalf of those who wait for him" (Isaiah 64:4)."The LORD is good to those whose hope is in him, to the one who seeks him; it is good to wait quietly for the salvation of the LORD" (Lamentations 3:25–26).

Yes, God does act on behalf of the one who waits for Him. God is good to the one who quietly waits. It was something that the women who waited in the upper room on that long ago day discovered. It is something we need to discover too.

A Closer Look at God's Truth

1. Read Luke 24:44–53; Acts 1:1–14. Just what exactly were the disciples told to wait for?

_____

_____

_____

_____

_____

_____

How long were they told to wait (Acts 1:5)?

_____

_____

_____

_____

_____

_____

What further insight do the following verses in John's Gospel give about what Jesus called "the gift my Father promised" (Acts 1:4)?

John 14:16–17, 26

_____

_____

_____

_____

_____

John 15:26–27

_____

_____

_____

_____

_____

John 16: 7–15

_____

_____

_____

_____

_____

_____

Although we're not waiting for the promise of the coming of the Holy Spirit in the same way the disciples were—He's here now—there is much we can learn from the attitude of those who waited. Immediately after Jesus's ascension, men and women gathered together in the upper room, in obedience to Christ's command, to wait for the promised Holy Spirit.

2. Reread Acts 1:12–14. In addition to the Eleven, who else was present in the upper room?

_____

_____

_____

_____

Describe the atmosphere of the room.

_____

_____

_____

_____

_____

What were all the people doing?

_____

_____

_____

_____

_____

_____

_____

The Upper Room

Upper rooms in Palestine were choice rooms. The wealthy often used them as living rooms, placed above the noise of busy city streets and away from the view of passersby. Sometimes the rooms were rented out and used as places of assembly, study, and prayer. Some of these rooms were large; the upper room in Acts 1:15 could accommodate 120 people.

It appears from the text that the room the disciples returned to after the ascension was well known to them. It was very likely the same upper room where they had celebrated the Passover meal before Jesus's crucifixion (Mark 14:12–16), perhaps even the room where He appeared to some of them after His resurrection (Luke 24:33–34; John 20:19, 26).

Women Who Wait

The reference to "the women" in Acts 1:14 is undoubtedly the same women mentioned in Luke 8:2–3; 23:49; 23:55—24:10. These women had followed Jesus throughout His ministry—even to the cross and the tomb. They also contributed finances from their own incomes to help support Him.

Acts 1:14 is the last direct reference made to Mary, Jesus's mother. Esteemed and honored though she was, after this she quietly disappears from history. That she is mentioned here is noteworthy. It means she was a witness to the change of heart experienced by her sons, Jesus's brothers, and that she was involved through prayer with the redemptive story of the New Testament—she was present when the church was birthed at Pentecost (Acts 2).

Jesus's Brothers Wait with Mary

During Jesus's ministry His brothers didn't believe in Him (John 7:3–5). They were offended at Him (Matthew 13:55–57; Mark 6:2–3) and thought He was out of his mind and perhaps even demon possessed (Mark 3:20–35).

3. What new information does Paul give about Jesus's brother James do you find in the following verses?
1 Corinthians 15:7

_____

_____

_____

_____

_____

_____

_____

_____

Galatians 2:9

_____

_____

_____

_____

_____

Acts 15:12–13

_____

_____

_____

_____

_____

The Bible does not tell us when or where Jesus appeared to James. James did become prominent in the early church and wrote the New Testament book of James. According to tradition James was martyred in AD 62.

Return now to Acts 1:14. This is the last mention made of Mary in the New Testament. We find her with the other women in the upper room. What might it have been like for Mary to have her sons present as they, now a part of that believing company, prayed and waited with her?

Have you ever prayed for someone for years and years before God answered your prayers? Tell about it.

_____

_____

_____

_____

_____

How did God's answer make you feel?

_____

_____

_____

_____

5. We are often called to pray and wait. Read the following verses and describe the kind of attitude God wants us to have as we wait for Him.

Psalm 27:14

_____

_____

_____

_____

_____

_____

Psalm 37:7

_____

_____

_____

_____

_____

_____

_____

Micah 7:7

_____

_____

_____

_____

_____

_____

Ways to Wait

In her book *Building Christian Discipline*, Eileen Pollinger suggests three ways in which we are to wait on the Lord: looking forward expectantly, holding back expectantly, and being ready and available.[1]

Looking forward expectantly is when we trust God to work in us and wait for His timing to act on our behalf. As we wait, we walk in obedience to His commands. We know He is going to do something in His perfect time, and we expectantly prepare ourselves for it.

Holding back expectantly is keeping our hands off and letting God work out the details of our problem. Realizing that our timing is often different from His, we don't try to outguess and outmaneuver Him. Instead we quietly wait for Him to lead the way.

Being ready and available is recognizing that although God's answer might not be for the "here and now," we still need to be ready when it comes. In the meantime we submit to God, continue to trust Him, and do what we can to prepare ourselves for His perfect time.

6. Read the parable Jesus told in Luke 15:11–24 from the viewpoint of the father in the story. How did he model the three aspects of waiting?

Looking forward expectantly

_____

_____

_____

_____

_____

_____

Holding back expectantly

_____

_____

_____

_____

Being ready and available

_____

_____

_____

_____

_____

_____

7. Read Psalm 5:3; Titus 2:13; James 1:5; 1 John 3:2. List some things to wait for as we look forward expectantly.

_____

_____

_____

_____

_____

_____

What should be taking place in our lives during this waiting time (Romans 12:1–2; 2 Timothy 2:15; Philippians 1:6)?

_____

_____

_____

_____

_____

_____

_____

Read Isaiah 8:17. What must we have in our relationship with God that will enable us to wait, holding back expectantly?

_____

_____

_____

_____

_____

_____

_____

Can you think of a time in your life when you had to wait by holding back expectantly? What did you do?

_____

_____

_____

_____

_____

_____

What happened as a result?

_____

_____

_____

_____

_____

_____

8. Read Ephesians 2:10. Why do we need to be ready and available?

_____

_____

_____

_____

_____

_____

_____

What can we do to be ready (Psalm 119:11; Matthew 6:24; Luke 11:1; Romans 12:6–8; 2 Timothy 2:15, 3:16)?

_____

_____

_____

_____

_____

_____

_____

_____

What does being available to God mean to you personally?

_____

_____

_____

9. Challenge activity: go back over the lives of the three Marys you have studied. Do any of these women model the three aspects of waiting—that of looking forward expectantly, holding back expectantly, being ready and available? Summarize your findings in your journal.

A Closer Look at My Life

A woman sent me the following note:

> I've been putting the three aspects of waiting to work in my marriage this week. (I've been praying about communication between me and my husband.) I can wait by looking forward expectantly as I read books on communication and by making an effort to spend quality time with him—like not turning the TV on as soon as I get home from work.
>
> I can hold back from calling attention to certain inadequacies I observe in him and choose never to criticize him publicly when he goofs. I can be ready and available to go with him to the car races or a football game. I can even get excited about looking at a new car.

10. This woman has taken a giant step in learning how to wait God's way. What about you? How can you apply what you've learned about waiting in your life?

_____

_____

_____

_____

_____

_____

What would you like to have happen in your life as a result of what you've learned?

_____

_____

_____

_____

_____

_____

_____

_____

_____

Action Steps I Can Take Today

11. A thought for you to ponder: Reread the story of Jesus's ascension into heaven in Acts 1:4–11. As you do, ask the Holy Spirit to show you if there is something that He specifically wants you to do. When He shows it to you, ask Him to give you the courage to wait, looking forward expectantly, holding back expectantly and being ready and available.

12. A prayer from your heart to the heart of your Father. *Heavenly Father, I'm waiting on you right now. I'm listening, wondering, even dreaming a little bit. How can I become a woman after your heart? A woman who loves, who serves, who bows in humble submission to your will?*

Lord, I know I can only be that kind of woman as I linger in your presence and ponder your ways. Teach me to trust you. Help me learn the disciplines of waiting so that I can teach others. And when I do, the glory will be yours, all yours, for I am your daughter. In Jesus's name. Amen.

13. As you complete this Bible study, remember this: you are called to be the daughter of a king. Like each of the three Marys, you have been invited to serve Him in unique and beautiful ways. "For it is by grace you have been saved, through faith—and this not from yourselves, it is the gift of God—not by works, so that no one can boast. For we are God's workmanship, created in Christ Jesus to do good works, which God prepared in advance for us to do" (Ephesians 2:8–10).

He is waiting for you to pour out on others the love He has poured out on you.

"The grace of the our Lord Jesus Christ be with you all. Amen" (Revelation 22:21 NKJV).

Notes

Lesson 7, "At the Empty Tomb"

1. Kenneth Barker, ed., *The NIV Study Bible* (Grand Rapids: Zondervan, 1995), 1585.

Lesson 8, "In the Upper Room

1. Eileen Pollinger, *Building Christian Discipline* (Bloomington, MN: Bethany House, 1986) 18.